101 Tips
for Preschool
at Home

Minimize Your Homeschool
Stress By Starting Right

How To Homeschool Series

Volume 1

ADRIANA ZODER

To my husband, for his love and support

Table of Contents

Acknowledgments...i

Introduction 1

Chapter 1: 10 Reasons I Embraced Homeschooling 3

Chapter 2: 10 Homeschooling Frequently Asked Questions...................11

Chapter 3: 10 Homeschool Essentials for Preschool at Home 17

Chapter 4: 10 Homeschooling Methods 23

Chapter 5: 10 Educational Objectives in Preschool 29

Chapter 6: 10 Educational Toys for Preschoolers 34

Chapter 7: 10 Preschool Curricula 39

Chapter 8: 10 Organizational Tips..45

Chapter 9: 10 Tips for Successful Field Trips...49

Chapter 10: 10 Reference Books for Home Educators...........................54

Chapter 11: Tip 101..60

Epilogue 63

About the Author...65

Review Request..66

ACKNOWLEDGMENTS

Soli Deo Gloria. Glory to God alone. This book would not exist if God did not call me to homeschool. I feel humbled that He considered me worthy of such a high calling.

Many thanks to Jose Agosto, PhD and Blondel Senior, PhD for reviewing the early drafts of this book.

Heartfelt appreciation goes toward my children, who teach me every day.

Last but not least, I am thankful to my husband for agreeing to homeschool.

INTRODUCTION

When you have small children and want to prepare to homeschool them, time is of the essence. Who has time for 250-page reference books which spell out homeschool philosophies and methodologies in detail? When your days and nights are blurry at best, you need sleep, not study hall.

This is where "101 Tips for Preschool at Home" comes in – a quick-start guide, solid enough to keep around as a reference book.

When I started researching homeschooling, my children were three and almost one. I read all these long homeschooling books through the foggy years of diapers, nighttime feedings, and potty training accidents. I made the effort because I was trying to come to grips with my new, surprising desire to teach my own.

My two children – a boy and a girl – taught me a lot, too. I studied and applied what seemed right for us, but much of the advice I read was for school-age children.

Through it all, I wished for a book to help me quickly understand what the preschool years were about, what homeschooling was, and how to find my own philosophy of education. To help others in the same situation, I wrote one myself.

The 101 tips I collected in this book go beyond theoretical principles, because education is a practical endeavor. George Bernard Shaw was simply having fun with words when he wrote, "Those who can't do, teach."

This book is organized in 10 chapters, each presenting 10 tips. Chapter 11 presents Tip 101, while the Epilogue shares a bonus tip about how to schedule your days.

Your parental love qualifies you to teach your preschooler. You can do it. This book can help you start the journey with confidence.

CHAPTER 1: 10 REASONS I EMBRACED HOMESCHOOLING

"All your children will be taught by the Lord, and great will be their peace." Isaiah 54:13

God talked to me gently about homeschooling. I refused to listen at first. He kept sending me messages about it through people, circumstances, books and – well – even the news.

Over time, saying "No" to God got exhausting. I was on the fence or, as a friend of mine put it, "in the valley of indecision." My husband and my friends got tired of listening to me arguing for and then immediately against homeschooling. After about two years, I gave in to God.

Once I said "yes" to God, many other reasons for

homeschooling came to mind. Isn't that always the case? Our faith wins the victory first. Then, our minds receive confirmation after confirmation that we are on the right path.

Here are 10 reasons why I embraced homeschooling:

1. I love God. He wants the best for me. I accept that His way is better than mine. I want to listen to His voice even when He calls me to take the road less traveled.

He has done it many times before. It's the story of my life. It has not been easy, but my conscience has been at peace.

2. The length of the school day in the USA means I would be separated from my children for seven hours a day. I have a hard time with that.

Before I had children, I did not think I would feel this way. But I do. I would wonder about their time away from me and miss them tremendously. I understand some parents must do this. I know it must be hard.

Since I grew up in Romania, I cannot wrap my mind around how American children spend 35 hours a week in school. If you add commute time, the "business" of attending school is a full time job. These children are "at it" since age five. Somehow I don't think childhood was supposed to be spent this way.

I used to go to school for four hours a day in elementary school, five hours in middle school, and six hours in high school. That was it. The amount of homework we received was not greater than what I hear American children bring home. And we received a rigorous education.

3. My private school of choice is one hour away.

Logistically, it would be impossible for me to enroll my child in a private school which is one hour away. But then, even if it were any closer, I would be baffled by the seven-hour school day (see previous point).

4. Public school teachers must present a godless worldview.

I don't blame them. It's just a fact. Public school teachers get paid to present a secular perspective.

Teaching other people's children is a noble and thankless job. While spending eight hours a day taking care of and teaching 25 children, the noise level alone stresses one out. Not to mention dealing with the children's attitudes, the discipline, and the special needs of each learner. I have a lot of respect for teachers' hard work.

In order to earn their salary, teachers must do their job, which includes staying neutral and politically correct when it comes to Bible truths or any other religious concepts.

I do not want my children exposed to a secular worldview for 35 hours a week. It would impact them too much.

5. *Harry Potter* and other books I don't want my children to read as required reading.

While my children were still toddlers, I asked a principal at a local elementary school if his students could read something else instead of *Harry Potter* or any other book I would disagree with. He said, "Yes, but it also depends on the teacher."

I did not want my children exposed to wizardry and/or paltry moral values through books. One teacher might be OK with replacing titles, but the next one might not.

6. Our home and our children's extracurricular activities provide better socialization than interacting with 25 (or more) peers for 35 hours a week.

Peer pressure would instill values I don't approve of in my children. This homeschooling mom told me she pulled her daughter out of public school after kindergarten. She had many reasons. One of her comments about peer pressure stuck with me. She said, "No more Justin Bieber parties for five-year-olds."

Last but not least, the geniuses of the human race spent very little time with their peers. (Susan Wise Bower, *The Well-Trained Mind*, p. 601)

How can I put this nicely? Spending almost 40 hours a week in the presence of other children your age does not exactly enhance your intellectual attainments.

7. Our children can pursue their interests after they get academics out of the way, which makes for a very efficient use of their time.

As we were discussing homeschooling with our pediatrician, he said his children went to public school and they just could not compete with homeschooled children when it came to playing an instrument or swimming, for instance.

A homeschooled student does not spend more than 4 hours a day on academics. Since the teacher-student ratio is a lot lower than in a traditional classroom, learning is efficient, too.

Then, he is free to jump in the pool or build LEGO models or practice his instrument for 4-7 hours a day, if he so chooses.

8. Public schools in my district test children using state standardized tests, not national standardized tests.

If I want my children to be competitive on a national scale, I need to know how they are doing on a national standardized test. We live in Tennessee, which is ranked toward the bottom among the United States in terms of educational attainments.

Even though our local school system is "exemplary" among Tennessee schools, it still has to test according to state standards.

As we homeschool, our children take national standardized tests instead.

9. I want my children to get all the sleep they need.

Growing children need lots and lots of sleep. Waking up at

7:00 so they can have breakfast and get dressed to jump in the car by 7:45 just does not seem like a nice way to start the day.

My children wake up naturally. We wake up naturally. We schedule appointments outside the home for the afternoons, if at all possible.

Of course I want them to understand that one day they might have a job that requires them to use an alarm clock. And we do have days when I have to wake them up so we can make an early appointment.

But while they are still very small, they must be allowed a full night's rest.

10. I did not want our morning routine to be a rush to get separated in four different directions.

They say that the family that prays together, stays together. They say that the family that has dinner together, stays together. Most statistics look at dinner because mainstream parents have lunch at work and traditionally schooled children have lunch at school. Breakfast does not even count, as many people skip breakfast altogether.

I relish our morning routine of waking up naturally and having a warm breakfast followed by a devotional time. Then, we do our chores, which we call morning cards (from the *Accountable Kids* program). Learning has already happened before we hit the books.

CHAPTER 2: 10 HOMESCHOOLING FREQUENTLY ASKED QUESTIONS

"Wisdom is the principal thing; therefore get wisdom: and with all thy getting, get understanding." Proverbs 4:7

1. What is homeschooling?

Homeschooling, also known as home education or home-based learning, happens when parents take the responsibility of their children's education upon themselves. They may hire tutors or do it themselves, or a combination. Homeschooling is no longer a fringe movement filled up with hippies or conservative Christian parents. A lot of parents these days in the USA, about two million according to some research sources, have decided to be the main guide of their children's education.

2. What is education?

Most people have never asked themselves this simple question. What does education look like? Does learning happen if a blackboard is not involved? What if you only have a classroom of one? Is that still education? Can learning happen only with a textbook present or are living (regular) books a good source of knowledge, as well?

These questions deserve an answer well thought out.

Education is the process of learning, not the process of going to a building called Something Something School. "Education is an atmosphere," in the words of Charlotte Mason, a British educator of the 19th century.

Homeschooling is about learning and not about schooling. Children learn in different ways. When you homeschool, you have the flexibility to choose certain schedules, methods and curricula that fit your child.

3. Is homeschooling legal in the United States?

Yes, it is. Homeschooling is legal in all fifty states. Different states have different homeschooling requirements though, so one must find their state support group and understand their state law. For instance, I live in Tennessee where the law requires homeschoolers to be registered under an "umbrella school" or with the local public school district. The umbrella schools in Tennessee simply keep your records. They do not teach classes. In California, an umbrella school has a completely different definition.

4. How should I register to homeschool in my state?

Go to the Homeschool Legal Defense Association's website www.hslda.org, and look for your state. From there, contact your state support organization and your local support group.

5. Am I depriving my preschooler of an educational experience if I don't put him in the most sought-after preschool in my town?

No, you are not. Research has shown that early childhood programs do not succeed in their goals. Loving parents who read to their small children and take them outside for play time do not need to worry about a formal preschool experience.

6. Will my child miss out on socialization if I don't put him in "the real world," i.e. a group setting with other children every day?

People have socialized their children in the context of home for millennia. Do you think American children were 'unsocialized' before 1852, when compulsory attendance was first introduced?

Socialization in a (pre)school environment is self-taught and unsupervised. This type of socialization has more to do with being cool and fitting in than with manners, team work, and being polite.

7. Will my homeschooled child do well on standardized tests?

Homeschooled children consistently score higher than their traditionally schooled peers on standardized tests. Some public school educators take offense to this statistics, but the truth is the truth: mothers without a college degree do a better job than certified teachers. There is something to be said about pouring motivation into a child through a loving, "I believe in you" attitude.

8. Will my homeschooled child get into college?

Colleges and universities accept and even seek out homeschool graduates. I personally know a homeschooler who got accepted to 10 out of 10 colleges she applied for and six of those offered her a full-ride scholarship.

When you homeschool through high school, you have time to do all those community service hours. You also have time to pursue your passions, whatever they may be.

And how about this one? You even have time for dual enrollment classes at a community college. You could graduate from high school and with an associate's degree by the time you are eighteen, saving your family tens of thousands of dollars in tuition, room and board.

9. What if I don't know much about a subject?

Luckily, you don't have to be an expert in everything in order to homeschool. Think of yourself as a facilitator of educational experiences. Once they can read, most children can teach themselves. You can also look into homeschool co-ops, support groups, online classes, video tutoring and dual enrollment classes at your local community college.

10. How much does it cost to homeschool?

Most people spend about $500 per child per year, but homeschooling can be done for a lot less or a lot more. A lot of it depends on your budget, goals, lifestyle, and educational methods.

CHAPTER 3: 10 HOMESCHOOL ESSENTIALS FOR PRESCHOOL AT HOME

"It is only with the heart that one can see rightly, what is essential is invisible to the eye." Antoine de Saint-Exupery

What do you really need to homeschool a preschooler? An early childhood education degree? Perfect bulletin boards? I blogged about five essentials on www.HomeschoolWays.com, but I expanded the list to a Top 10 because, well, when it comes to essentials, more is more.

Here is my Top 10 list of homeschool essentials:

1. A supportive husband – oh where, oh where do I begin on

this one? Many of us get married to the man of our dreams. I did.

A few years into our marriage, motherhood changed me. I wanted to – horrors! - homeschool the children. My husband was not keen on the idea.

I prayed. If this was indeed God's calling on me, He would convince my husband. I sure tried and failed to convince him of the benefits of homeschooling. So it was all up to God.

What do you know? God changed my husband's heart. He is now the proud principal of our homeschool.

A supportive husband can let you vent, help you figure things out, pray with you for the children, pray for you, rejoice with you, cry with you, bring a tissue box when you cry, keep the kids while you take a walk through the neighborhood, discipline the children when you are too angry to do a fine job at it, use common sense when you are out of it, etc etc etc. A supportive husband is invaluable and the first and foremost essential.

2. A library card – Save your money for curriculum and/or field trips by getting 90% of your books from the library. I downloaded reading lists from www.SimplyCharlotteMason.com or the 1000 Good Book List from www.classical-

homeschooling.org. My local library either had the titles or they got them for me through the inter-library loan program.

I started my children with trips to the library when they were in diapers. We also attended Story Time and Summer Reading Programs, where my children learned to sit down and be quiet, or interact with other children when allowed.

3. A support group – Local homeschooling support groups will hold your hand through thick and thin. Take advantage of the generosity of these experienced moms who are willing to counsel and share their knowledge.

Like-minded friends and their children will, in some cases, become closer to you than your own family, especially if your family is against homeschooling.

Whether for birthday parties or weekly play dates, homeschooling friends provide the kind of socialization that mothers of preschoolers want and need.

Small children parallel play for the first three years of their lives, but then they really enjoy playing with other children once they get to be four and five. Mothers talk while their children play together. Everybody wins.

4. An internet connection – It is impossible to do research at the library while keeping an eye on small children. My online research happens at night, after I put the children to bed. If you can afford an internet connection at home, it is well-worth it, especially when you live far from your local library. Not only can you gain inspiration from homeschooling blogs, you can save money by purchasing used curriculum on www.HomeschoolClassifieds.com and by taking advantage of the world's largest retail store, www.Amazon.com.

5. Craft materials – You may want to splurge on some items and skimp on others. But paint, glue, construction paper, scissors, and crayons are essentials. Kids learn a lot of skills through crafts and should be allowed the freedom to create and make something with their hands.

6. Park with playground – Your preschoolers will need lots of time outdoors to develop gross motor skills and to expand all that energy. If the weather allows it, you might want to schedule a daily stop by the playground. It helps everybody sleep better.

7.   Zoo/Aquarium/Children's   museum   membership – Depending on where you live, you might want to invest in one of these annual memberships. This will give you a place to take your children regardless of the weather outside. We have memberships at the Knoxville Zoo and Ripley's Aquarium in Gatlinburg. The Zoo offered an indoor play area with small animals, but also all sorts of educational toys.

Over time, we found that we could only go to one consistently. Guess which one? The one that was closest to us, the Aquarium. So we let the Zoo membership lapse and got it renewed only when we knew we wanted to go back to it.

8. The Old Schoolhouse Magazine, found online at www.TheHomeschoolMagazine.com – free and digital, this magazine will give you all the information you need to stay abreast of legal news, educational methodology, and the latest homeschool products. This helpful, informative, and inspirational magazine also operates www.SchoolhouseTeachers.com, an online co-op for the price of a regular co-op membership. Bonus: flexible teaching hours, over 50 courses to choose from, and no commute time.

9. Building toys – LEGO bricks can be introduced at four, but please be careful. Four-year-olds typically have younger siblings in diapers who put everything in their mouths. Even five-year-olds put things in their mouths. I know because I have caught my own in the act. While he knew better than to swallow, it still frightened me because he could do so by accident.

10. A reliable car for mom and children – I have friends who homeschool and own only one car. It can be done, no question about it. But if your children take classes outside the home, a reliable second car in the family becomes a homeschool essential.

A second car for mom and children also makes it possible to take field trips and run errands while daddy is at work.

CHAPTER 4: 10 HOMESCHOOLING METHODS

"She was wise, subtle, and knew more than one way to skin a cat."
Mark Twain, *A Connecticut Yankee in King Arthur's Court*

Homeschooling is different for every family. Many find themselves loving one curriculum or one approach, yet others may fall in the "eclectic" category, where they blend several approaches as needed.

Don't worry if you don't understand some of the educational lingo or concepts at first. Keep reading and studying and applying the things you do connect with. Over time, your experience will teach you which approach you should take.

For all practical purposes, I have grouped homeschooling

approaches or methods into 10 different categories.

1. Classical – A child's brain development naturally sets the stage for the trivium, the core concept in a classical education. The trivium is made up of three stages: primary school, or the grammar stage, during which learning is based on concrete tasks and memorizing facts; middle school or the logic stage, during which learning tackles abstract concepts and reasoning from cause to effect; and high school or the rhetoric stage, when learning focuses more on expressing what has already been acquired. This is the method I lean toward heavily because a) I learned this way and b) it makes sense.

2. Charlotte Mason – A British educator of the nineteenth century, Ms. Mason is more relevant today than ever, in my opinion. Her emphasis on living books, i.e. regular books (as opposed to textbooks/workbooks), narration (the child telling you back the story you just read to him), and nature study would bring life to any educational pursuit. I like this approach very much and use it to balance my natural propensity toward rote memorization. If you decide this is the approach you like, you can even get free curriculum at www.AmblesideOnline.com, with a Charlotte Mason

emphasis. All you have to do is borrow the books from the library.

3. Unit Studies – The method which took me the most to understand and appreciate, even though I studied under and worked with one of its biggest proponents, Dr. Raymond Moore. The Prussian educational method of separating knowledge into subjects, used in public schools, indoctrinated, er... trained me well. Once I got unit studies though, I used Before Five in a Row and came to a new level of freedom in my mind about home education. The mother of all unit study curricula is Konos. I find I am not brave enough for it, but it obviously works for a great number of homeschoolers.

4. Traditional – Most of us learned like this in a public school somewhere around the world. Textbooks provide the theory, which you apply while filling out workbooks. Homeschoolers tend to call this method dry and boring, but some children thrive on this method. I have a three-year old who asks for worksheets almost every day. Rod and Staff, Abeka and Bob Jones are examples of traditional curricula. Personally, I have used Rod and Staff and anything I can find online. There is a vast array of worksheets online. Don't get overwhelmed.

5. Unschooling – Also known as relaxed homeschooling or delight-based or child-led. I could not be an unschooler, but I like the emphasis on the child's desire to look into a certain topic. I recognize that the highest point of learning is when a child asks a question though. So I capitalize on those teaching moments throughout the day. However, I need the structure of a schedule and a carefully laid out curriculum to feel sane.

6. Eclectic – People like me, who pick and choose at least two different methods, curricula and approaches to tailor the education of their children, are called eclectic homeschoolers. In other words, if you are not a purist when it comes to one particular method, you may be an eclectic homeschooling parent.

7. Montessori – Maria Montessori's "let-the-child-lead-the-way" approach to education set in motion a wonderful network of Montessori schools all over the world. No spiritual component makes this method adaptable to whatever religion is celebrated in the home.

8. Waldorf – Very similar to Montessori's gentle approach, the Waldorf method differs in that it emphasizes anthroposophy – the belief that people must first understand humanity before understanding the workings of the universe. A Waldorf education follows the philosophy of Rudolf Steiner.

9. Independent study and online schools – Many parents find that their children respond well to studying online or with DVDs. Landry Academy, Abeka DVDs or Switched-On Schoolhouse from Alpha-Omega Publications fit in this category.

10. The Moore Formula – For a balanced education, i.e. one which trains the hand, the heart and the head, taking into consideration a child's readiness level for formal education, I always keep in mind The Moore Foundation's philosophy. In fact, it is the overarching method I use before making any decision in my homeschool.

The two most important aspects of the Moore Formula are delayed academics and unit studies. What Dr. Raymond Moore postulated was that, when it comes to formal academics, it is better late than early. And when you teach, you should use the unit study approach. Thus, your child will see how different subjects connect.

CHAPTER 5: 10 EDUCATIONAL OBJECTIVES IN PRESCHOOL

"Let the child's first lesson be obedience, and the second will be what thou wilt." Benjamin Franklin

1. Obedience – Absolutely, this is your number one objective in preschool. You cannot go anywhere until your preschooler respects you and your words.

2. Appreciation for nature as God's creation – Time spent outdoors will benefit your preschooler physically, emotionally, intellectually and spiritually. Studies have shown that youngsters

who play outside do better in science, for instance. But, beyond that, you have the privilege of introducing your young child to the Creator, the Author of all the beauty in the natural world.

3. Helping at home – Small children love helping mom and dad around the house, but their efforts tend to hinder at this stage. What's a busy mom to do? Use your judgment. If they play happily by themselves, put the laundry in the washing machine without their help or start cooking or do whatever else needs to be done around the house.

If, on the other hand, they show an interest as they see you working, by all means let them "help" you. It's a slow process, but they will become such responsible adults because of it.

4. Music appreciation – Turn music on as you drive from point A to point B, as children play quietly, or as you share family meals together. Over time, they will start asking questions and develop an ear for different composers.

5. Introduction to family's religious values – Start them young, they say. What a privilege we have to bring our children to Jesus

every day. I used to read the Bible story of the mothers who brought their children to Jesus and did not realize it applied to me, too. I could bring my children into Jesus' presence by singing appropriate children's songs, by reading simple Bible stories and by helping them put together a Bible craft. That's it. It's not rocket science and you do not need a theology degree.

6. Caring for one's body – These are the days of potty learning and washing hands before meals. Also, during the preschool years, parents can start teaching their children about healthy foods vs. non-healthy foods and about the dangers of smoking, drinking and illegal drugs. Studies show that eight-year-olds have already decided whether they would like to smoke one day. So you must catch them before that, obviously, and teach them diligently.

Sex education should also start around age four. Teach them what is an acceptable touch and that they should not have secrets with anybody. They must tell you everything that anybody does to them.

Also, they must know to say loudly, "No. Don't do this. I will tell my parents." Predators stay away from children who protest, who are not submissive, and who will tell somebody if they get touched inappropriately.

Better yet, never allow your children to be alone with anybody, under any circumstance, for any length of time. Easier said than done, but possible.

7. Getting along with siblings – Teamwork represents an invaluable life skill and what better place to learn it than in the family, with siblings? You have, no doubt, seen the T-shirt which proclaims, "Does not play well with others."

Bickering will happen. It's a fact of life. We will always have sibling rivalry. That is our opportunity to teach our children how to get along and play well with others.

8. Reading time is fun time – I have read to my children since they were a couple weeks old. We started out with one board book a day and grew to three picture books by the time they were preschoolers.

Your goal should be 20 minutes of reading a day. They learn that books equal adventures and the cuddle times with loving parents will remain a cherished memory for the rest of their lives.

9. Gardening is the ABC of education – You don't have to be a full-time farmer to introduce your children to the amazing process of growing food. You don't even have to be an expert.

I have never had a green thumb, having grown up in a city. But since I became a mom, I started planting a 4'x8' parcel in the backyard with vegetable seedlings. They don't always turn out well. However, we have lots of fun in the sun and dirt as we water and weed. And the kids take pride in "their" garden.

If you live in a city, potted plants will do just fine. You will be surprised by how much you can grow if you are willing. Lessons of character training, math, science and language arts abound as you tend to the plants.

10. Service – Visiting elderly neighbors or nursing home residents, writing cards for a sick relative, picking up trash around the neighborhood, baking cookies for others, and making a craft for somebody else are all examples of service opportunities.

Children must learn from an early age that the world does not revolve around them. We need to show them the rewards of helping others for no material return. Kindness comes back.

CHAPTER 6: 10 EDUCATIONAL TOYS FOR PRESCHOOLERS

"Growing up, I didn't have a lot of toys, and personal entertainment depended on individual ingenuity and imagination – think up a story and go live it for an afternoon." Terry Brooks, author of 23 New York Times best-selling fantasy fiction books

Most, if not all toys for preschoolers should have no batteries. Here are the best educational toys for the preschool years, in no particular order:

1. DUPLO brick sets – The best construction toy, these

DUPLO sets even come with lesson plans if you look at LEGO Education. But a simple 100-brick starter kit should keep any preschooler happy for a long, long time.

2. An Easel - We used to have an inexpensive easel and our children outgrew it in size. Plus, they somehow managed to break the chalkboard side. I don't think we ever knew how it happened. It's one of those things children do and parents scratch their heads.

So, we decided to invest in a better one. Since we have hardwood floors, we added felt pads to each leg. Then, we bought butcher paper, i.e. lots of it. We might still have this by the time they get into high school, and that is just fine. We saved all kinds of money by buying this 900' roll from Amazon.

Our kids spend precious minutes painting, drawing, and doodling on this. We can use it in three ways: on the chalkboard side with chalk, on the white board side with dry erase markers, and on the white board side with the butcher paper (the clips come in handy to block the paper in place).

3. Sort and Snap Color Match by Melissa & Doug – My daughter received this for her second birthday and played a lot with it. When she got tired of it, I put it up and brought it back out

a month later. It's a classic toy and it has grown with our daughter.

At two, it was more about gross motor skills – getting the snaps into their holes. Then, around three, it was about matching colors. Finally, as she matured into a sophisticated four-year-old, she wanted to use the black-and-white side of the designs and make her own colorful designs.

4. Pattern Blocks and Boards by Melissa & Doug – My son was in kindergarten when we started doing a math lesson on patterns. My daughter, only three at the time, wanted to work on patterns as well. I found this great set and she loved playing with it. Sometimes, it kept her busy for 30 minutes.

The boards have two designs, one on each side. Both the boards and the blocks are sturdy. I keep the blocks in a zip-lock bag, inside the big box where the boards are nested. Both my children play with the blocks even without the boards. They create designs and patterns of their own. These blocks can also be used to teach colors, counting, shapes, and addition.

5. 100-Piece Wood Block Set by Melissa & Doug – My son received this for Christmas when he was only one. Every year, we sort through our toys and decide what they have outgrown and

what can stay. This set never even comes close to the outgoing pile. It is a mainstay.

Wood blocks grow with your child. I have watched my babies stack two blocks, then three, then four. As toddlers, they took great pleasure in building and tearing down. As preschoolers, they built trucks, elaborate towers and even planes. Of course, one can learn colors, shapes and counting with these. Hand-eye coordination, too. We even use them in our Bible stories sometimes.

6. Deluxe Wooden Stringing Beads by Melissa & Doug – I'll be honest with you, I did not need another set with small parts around the house. But this toy is not only cute, it is very good for improving fine motor skills. So, I gave in. It has been a great success with our daughter.

She was almost four when we got it for her. I had to spend some time with her in the beginning, to teach her how to do it and show her some possibilities. Eventually, she moved into a more independent phase in playing with this set.

7. Puzzles – From giant size cardboard pieces to wooden pieces with small handles, puzzles come in many shapes and sizes. Your preschooler's puzzles can feature their favorite stories:

Madeleine, Dr. Seuss, animals, you name it.

8. Balls of various sizes to roll, kick, bounce, throw, and catch with parents, siblings, and friends.

9. Tricycle and/or bicycle – Riding toys represent one of the best memories of a childhood spent well, outdoors, enjoying fresh air and sunshine as the weather allows.

10. Corn toss and other similar tossing games which provide not just fun, but also a chance to improve hand-eye coordination.

CHAPTER 7: 10 PRESCHOOL CURRICULA

"It is a miracle that curiosity survives formal education." Albert Einstein

The best curriculum you could follow is your preschooler's curiosity. Answer her questions, take her to the library, on nature walks, on various field trips, and let her explore.

An excellent preschool experience can also include worksheets if your preschooler shows an interest. I'm all for delayed academics and a gentle introduction to seat work. On the other hand, I believe in allowing the child's curiosity to lead the way. If you have a preschooler who is curious about "doing school," by all means provide a bit of pen and paper work for her.

My three-year-old daughter, spurred on by seeing her older brother "do school," started asking to "do math" every day. So I had to give her a few minutes a day of workbook activities. As soon as she got bored, we stopped.

Here are 10 programs we have used and enjoyed:

1. Rod and Staff publishes simple, solid workbooks for the preschool set. They are black and white. Cutting, pasting, coloring, matching, tracing – it's all there.

a. Rod and Staff Activity Workbooks for 4- and 5-year-olds – My daughter was three when she worked through these books. While she did not do everything perfectly, it provided a good beginning for her work with pen and paper, scissors and glue. She wanted to do it, too. Otherwise I would not have bought this set.

b. Rod and Staff Activity Workbooks for 4- and 5-year-olds – When my son was five and in kindergarten, I put these books in front of him, but they were too easy for him. His younger sister inherited them by default. When she finished the four booklets mentioned under 1.a. above, she started working through this set and loved it just as much.

2. Alpha Omega Publications Horizons Preschool Curriculum (for 3- and 4-year-olds) – I ordered this for my daughter when she was four. She wanted to learn with pen and paper so much – as opposed to my son, my firstborn, who was a hands-on learner.

This program is Christian, colorful, cute and very thorough, without burning your preschooler out. The resource materials can be used over and over as you work with other curricula, too.

Even though they expect four-year-olds to start printing, you can ignore that part and focus on all the other activities – the same is true about any other printable or workbook you get for this age.

3. *Singapore Mathematics, Earlybird Kindergarten, Book A* – A four-year-old would probably be able to work through most of this book. My son worked through this book at five going on six and he was bored. A great, solid resource, with not too much busy work, to keep your preschool student from getting overwhelmed.

4. *Before Five in a Row* (BFIAR) – Although the publishers will tell you BFIAR is not a curriculum, I consider it as such and many people do. I used it when my daughter was two going on three and my son was four going on five. We had so much fun.

BFIAR is a collection of unit studies based on picture books for young children. You do not need to buy the books you will be reading. Your local library should have most of them or they can procure them for you through the inter-library loan program.

5. www.HandsOfAChild.com – Lapbooks deserve a special place in your homeschool. Preschoolers love to cut and paste. The songs are charming. I felt some of the subjects were over my children's heads, so we worked on simple lapbooks about fall, winter, spring and the colors of the rainbow, for instance. If you watch the website for sales, especially in August, you can get a lot of lapbooks for half the price.

6. *Slow and Steady, Get Me Ready* by June Oberlander – Even a super-busy mom of preschoolers and toddlers and babies can handle this book. One activity per week from birth to age five prepares your children for kindergarten learning. I worked through it with my children and we enjoyed it a lot. At age four, they introduce letters (manuscript) and numbers, which might be too much for some children.

7. *A Year in Art* by Prestel Publishing – I cannot say enough about this art devotional. A painting a day, with room to record your thoughts, can give your preschoolers just enough exposure to the greatest paintings of the world and lay the foundation gently for art appreciation as adults. We use it during our afternoon tea time. The locations spur us on to open the atlas and discover where Delft or Louveciennes are, for instance. For your information, the book does contain paintings featuring the nude body.

8. Classical music CDs and/or a www.Pandora.com account – Quality classical and sacred music does not have to be expensive. Create your own channel on Pandora and you only have to put up with a few commercials now and then, which, of course, can be used as another learning opportunity for children.

9. *My Bible Friends* by Etta B. Degering – We read these books during the day and then the children listened to the CDs before going to bed. Soon, they knew entire sentences by heart. I, too, learned a lot, as I listened to the intonation of professional story-tellers.

10. *My Bible Story Book* by Charlotte F. Lessa – Caution! You might read through this book for an hour at a time and never stop. The illustrations hold the attention of small children, while the story line simplifies complex Bible concepts. As we finish one story, my children point to the next page and ask for more.

CHAPTER 8: 10 ORGANIZATIONAL TIPS

"Let all things be done decently and in order." 1 Corinthians 14:40

1. *Born to Win* by Zig Ziglar is one of the best books you will ever read on organizing your life. Planning, accomplishing goals and finding which goals you should focus on, based on your understanding of God's will for your life, it's all there. From the high-power executive to the patient homeschooling mom, all may benefit from this small but concept-filled book which will challenge you in classic Ziglar style.

2. *The 12-Week Year* by Brian Moran will take you to the next

level in productivity. By planning your goals quarterly, instead of annually, you get pushed to accomplish more than you ever thought possible. Measuring execution plays a big role, as well as weekly assessment and planning sessions. They even have an online program that can calculate your percentages weekly. As long as you execute 85% or more of your weekly goals, you are on target for your quarterly goals.

3. *Getting Things Done* by David Allen remains a classic in organization principles. Some of the software tools suggested may be dated, but you can still benefit from the core ideas of the book, like the 2-minute rule, the 43 folders, and the Drive-Your-Inbox-to-Zero approach. But the most important benefit from reading this book in my estimation is learning how to think about your goals without stressing over them.

4. "Early to bed, early to rise" is more than just a quaint old saying. I realize there are night owls among us. But even night owls can use some beauty sleep. Try getting to bed 30 minutes earlier compared to last week and reap the benefits of sleep that happens before midnight. If you just can't fall asleep, maybe you need more physical activity during the day.

5. Every six months, spring clean your home and your homeschool supplies. You will be surprised by how much you can throw out, donate or sell. Weekly, you should show your home love by vacuuming, dusting and cleaning the bathrooms. Daily, you should have a 10-minute pick-up-the-room session. Involve your preschooler by making it a race against the clock. "How much can you and mommy pick up in 10 minutes?" Teach your preschooler the rule, "If you take it, you put it back."

6. Use a planner – if nothing more than a large calendar by the phone in the kitchen. When you are out and about and somebody asks you if you can do something on such and such a date, you can say, "I don't know. I have to go home and check my calendar." It gives you an easy way out of a hasty commitment, too.

7. Check out www.DonnaYoung.org for free planning forms. Try not to be overwhelmed. I know I was, at first. I went back to it several times and found what I needed, but the diversity of those forms took my breath away. You might want to wait until you know what you need before going there. Or, go there to learn what is available. You don't have to make a decision right away.

8. Set aside 10 minutes every evening, after your children have gone to bed, to review materials for the next day.

9. Take time for a weekly review. What did you do well? What needs improvement? What do you need to prepare for this coming week? You might have to purchase some supplies, print and laminate resources, or talk to people for certain projects coming up soon.

10. If you live in a state where you must show for four hours daily, you will want to get in the habit of jotting down what you accomplished that day. You don't have to be consistent throughout the preschool years, of course, as nothing is official yet. But it helps to figure out what kind of recording system would suit you.

CHAPTER 9: 10 TIPS FOR SUCCESSFUL FIELD TRIPS

"Never go on trips with anyone you do not love." Ernest Hemingway

Somebody told me once that, while courting, young couples should take at least one trip together, so that they may discover who they really are. I believe there is much truth to that and, in fact, I have applied this advice.

But now, you have these amazing children whom you adore. Taking a trip together should feel like paradise, right? Right. If you are prepared, that is. If you are not prepared, your trip can turn into a nightmare very quickly.

So here are 10 things you should consider if you want a successful field trip with your children:

1. Check the weather prognosis the night before and dress accordingly. After a front of cooler weather last August, I figured I should wear long sleeves and long pants for our TVA Fair field trip. If I had known it was going to be 80F, I would have worn shorts and short sleeves.

If your field trip is mainly outdoors on a sunny day, use sunscreen and re-apply every two hours. Wear wide-brimmed hats. Pack rain gear - think small umbrellas or ponchos - if it's overcast or over 20% chance of showers.

2. Download and print a venue map and schedule from their website. Familiarize yourself with the entrance(s), exit(s) and bathroom locations. These days, terrible things happen in malls, museums, movie theaters, and other benign public places. Have the map handy while you walk around. You don't want to have to dig for it should an emergency occur.

Do they close for lunch? Do they close for cleaning and then re-open one hour later? If so, what does it take to get back inside?

The TVA Fair closed down the rides between 3-4pm. If I had known about it, we would have ridden a few rides first and only then would we have had our picnic.

But I did not, so we picnicked and then found out we could not ride. My five-year-old understood, but my three-year-old did not. She cried loudly and refused to be comforted. I could have spared her that if I had prepared better.

3. Check your gas tank and put the umbrella stroller in the car the night before. This may sound like a no-brainer, but, when you have small children, a detail like this can easily slip through the cracks. I've been there, done that.

4. Pack changes of clothes and shoes for the children and for yourself. Children spill drinks all the time, sometimes on mommy.

5. Bring your children's stuffed animals, travel pillows, some look-through/reading materials, as well as crayons and drawing pads. If you get stuck in traffic or if your destination is more than twenty minutes away, your children need to be occupied in the car. Mine like to thumb through picture books and doodle.

The stuffed animals provide security and comfort. The pillows don't have to be new or especially kept for car trips. You can use their regular pillows. My children do not take a nap anymore at the house, but, occasionally, they fall asleep in the car. A pillow comes in handy to support their heads.

6. Play CDs with stories, classical music or foreign languages. Do not underestimate car schooling.

7. Explain to the children ahead of time what the schedule will look like. If there is a gift shop and you do not want to buy anything, tell them so before you get there. Some places make you exit through the gift shop. When your children start asking for a cute stuffed pink octopus, you can remind them (and yourself) of your previous conversation.

8. Give yourself fifteen extra minutes to get to your destination. Arriving on time means you are actually late. Especially when you have to unload a stroller and get all your small children out of the car, walk from the parking lot to the entrance, connect with your group, use the bathrooms, change a

diaper etc etc etc. Not to mention getting stuck in traffic, which is possible at any time of the day.

9. Ditch the purse. Carry a backpack instead. Here's what you should put in it:

a. your camera – your phone camera may be fine, but in some instances you may want to film or you may need a flash; your phone may or may not be equipped with those features.

b. cash – you never know what can happen and/or if they take credit cards.

c. business/mommy cards - sometimes you will meet new homeschooling moms on a field trip. It is hard to write down a phone number while supervising children running around.

d. the coordinator's phone number, if on a group field trip.

10. Pray before, during and after the trip, especially if you see everybody getting tired and cranky. Watch your attitude. Your children will imitate you. If you are enthusiastic, they will be, too.

CHAPTER 10: 10 REFERENCE BOOKS FOR HOME EDUCATORS

"The giving of love is an education in itself." Eleanor Roosevelt

So here you are, thinking about homeschooling. No greater love exists, according to the Lord Jesus, than to lay down one's life for another. When you put 15-20 years into homeschooling your children, you lay down your life for them. You choose to forgo the pleasures and fulfillment of a career outside the home in order to give your children your time, your person, your love, your energy.

The experience of giving all this love is an education in itself, according to the quote above. And so, as you empty yourself, you will need to refuel on a regular basis. Somebody recommended I read a good reference book a summer, but I found I needed to read such books year-round. You decide what is right for you.

Here are the 10 best reference books I found:

1. *The Ultimate Guide to Homeschooling* by Debra Bell – Lots of good information for the beginner homeschooling mom. It will help you relax about the whole concept of homeschooling, too, as it breaks it all down and shows you how to do it. It encourages you over and over again to not bring school home. Homeschooling is not about schooling, it is about learning.

2. *The Moore Formula Manual* by Dr. Raymond and Dorothy Moore – A great resource to have on hand as you make decisions based on solid educational principles like delayed academics, unit studies, and allowing the child to be involved in his own education.

3. *The Well-Trained Mind* by Susan Wise Bower– A quality curriculum guide through high school, not just for those who seek after a classical education. A lot of the titles recommended in this book will serve your family no matter which approach you take.

4. *For the Children's Sake* by Susan Shaeffer Macaulay – This book soothes me. It's not a devotional. But it soothes me. It is a magnificent treaty on how true education builds a person up on every aspect of their being. The writer shows Charlotte Mason principles and how they apply in a practical way.

Especially for those of us who grew up with rough-around-the-edges, less-than-ideal public (or private) school environments, this book will show a different way. Your children will call themselves blessed for having a parent like you, if you implement these principles into your homeschool.

5. *Teaching Preschoolers* by Ruth Beechick – If you don't get anything else, get this book to learn about the preschooler's mind and the kind of expectations you can have. Dr. Beechick presents educational theories and lingering myths about the different aspects of the preschool years. More importantly, she shows how to strike a balance between contradicting educational theories.

The first chapters in the book deal with theories and myths about the preschool-age child, while the rest of the chapters give you practical suggestions for your homeschool. In that sense, this book alone could give you a guide as to what curriculum to do at home with your little scholars.

And here's my tip: read the book once, then work with your preschooler for six months. Then, re-read the book. You will get her points even more after having worked with your child, and having seen for yourself the kind of challenges or concepts she writes about.

6. *101 Top Picks for Homeschool Curriculum* by Cathy Duffy – Every homeschooler should have this book on their reference shelf. The first few chapters explain methods and learning styles. You will walk away with a clearer picture of what your homeschool should be like.

7. *Ten Ways to Destroy the Imagination of Your Child* by Anthony Esolen – Are you tired of the politically correct messages about rearing children, coming at you from parenting magazines and other media? Esolen shows you everything that is wrong with today's methods of caring for children. Thankfully, he also provides solutions. This book will not only open your eyes, it will entertain you, as the author can be quite funny.

8. *The Homeschool Mom's Bible* (KJV or NIV) – The

devotional portion of this Bible was written by Janet Tatman. It is also available for free on the Alpha-Omega Publications website, as a year-long devotional book, or as an eBook. I like this convenient way to look texts up right there, in the Bible, as I read the devotional.

Personally, I read several devotionals in a day. I don't have to follow the calendar and, besides, I need a lot of spiritual food and concepts to mull over as I prepare for the homeschooling trenches of each day. I can't just read one day at a time, as I would have to, should I only go to the free version, online.

I find Janet's writing very accessible and just right for my level. I know some people have complained that she even supplies a prayer at the end of the devotional. Guess what? Some of us, who are still earning our stripes in homeschooling, don't even know what to pray for sometimes. These prayers show us how we should tackle the issues that might pop up in the future.

9. *A Charlotte Mason Companion* by Karen Andreola – The Bible on Charlotte Mason, if you will. The purple book that will inspire any mother looking to instill in their children that education is a way of life.

10. *A Handbook of Nature Study* by Anna Comstock – Whether you follow the Charlotte Mason method or not, you will need a reliable nature study guide and this is it. Don't be fooled by its first publication date (1911). Trees and animals, rocks and minerals have not changed all that much since. The details in the book will guide you in teaching your students a lot or just a little, depending on their level of interest. I especially like the questions at the end of each study unit. They can be used as a curriculum.

CHAPTER 11: TIP 101

"The Christian life is not a constant high. I have my moments of deep discouragement." Billy Graham

If Billy Graham's Christian life was not a constant high, you can expect your homeschooling years will not be a constant high, either. You will get discouraged. You will feel like a failure. You will be tempted to give up and hail the yellow school bus the next day. You will want to quit at least once a year (usually, during winter). You will think about calling the local school district as soon as they open. You will find yourself doing research on private schools available within a 20-mile radius from your house.

A wise man told me once, "Never make decisions when you are discouraged. Wait until you recover emotionally and then pray harder than ever for wisdom and discernment."

Please don't go into homeschooling thinking that you will always feel the enthusiasm and spiritual high you were on when you first accepted God's call. Homeschooling is like anything else in life. You will have ups and downs. You will need grit. Courage. Perseverance. And many other things.

Your best weapon against discouragement? Prayer. This is Tip 101. It's not the last tip. It's the most important one, in a category of its own. I have saved the best for last.

Here's the good news: nobody knows your children like God. He gave them to you and now you need to go back to Him daily to find out how to guide them. Never forget He has promised to give you wisdom if you ask.

Prayer comes in many forms:

a. A desperate prayer as you discover your toddler may have been playing with dangerous chemicals.

b. A morning prayer, while all your household is asleep, and you are gathering your thoughts for the day.

c. An evening prayer, reviewing the events of the day,

thanking God for victories, big or small, or confessing sins of impatience and lack of graciousness toward your children.

d. A mid-day prayer, during your afternoon walk or quiet time, wondering if you should ask your kindergartener to re-do his copy work or let it be since, after all, he is only six and doing his best.

e. A middle of the night prayer, when you lie awake and cannot go back to sleep because of tensions you feel mounting between your children.

f. A prayer during family devotions, for a friend who asked you to pray that her son may change his mind about joining the Army.

g. A prayer with your spouse regarding a character trait in your children which you would like to see nipped in the bud.

A praying mother is a powerful agent for good not only in her household, but also in the world. It helps to have a prayer notebook to jot prayers and answers in. Whether you have a Prayer tab in your Planner Binder, or a notebook dedicated only to prayers, writing down your prayers and God's answers will inspire you.

EPILOGUE

Flying high on the wings of the philosophy of education can only take you so far. Sooner or later, we all must come back down to terra ferma, i.e. the nitty-gritty of teaching. Make no mistake about it. Teaching is doing.

In the words of a beginner homeschooling mom, "What do I DO?" This mom, whom I know personally, happened to have a master's in education and several years of classroom experience. When her child developed severe joint pains due to anxiety stemming out of a highly competitive academic environment, the parents had to pull her out of this "perfect little Christian school."

This mother and career educator never dreamed she would one day homeschool her child. In spite of all her training, degrees, and experience, she had no clue where to start, either.

If you, too, are trying to come up with a daily schedule, I suggest you use the "Schedule with Anchors" principle, from the Moore Formula Manual.

What are anchors, I hear you ask? Anchors are activities one does every day: meals, family devotions, personal hygiene, mail and newspaper pickup, laundry, pick-up-the-room times, wake-up routine, bedtime routine etc.

Ready? Take a piece of paper and put down your three meals and all the other activities you know you must accomplish every day and the approximate time they happen at. You will see then the remaining time you have on hand to slide in the rest of your goals.

Preschool at home is not rocket science. And if you experience low-energy days, don't fret. Just take care of the anchors and let your kids be kids. Children need a lot of time to play and come up with their own games and toys. They need freedom. Make sure you give them lots of unscheduled time for free play.

Through it all, bring your family in prayer before God and allow Him to guide you. Rest in His love, in the assurance that He Who called you is faithful and will finish what He started in and around you.

Homeschooling can be such a blessing not just to your family, but to the people whose lives will cross your paths and the paths of your children.

My prayers are with you.

ABOUT THE AUTHOR

Born in Romania under Communism, Adriana Zoder was a teenager when the Berlin Wall fell.

She studied French and English at the University of Bucharest in Romania and Publications Management at Hartland College in the United States.

After living in Sweden for three years, Adriana returned to the United States, where she worked in non-profit, educational foundations and, more recently, in real estate.

Since 2011, Zoder has been writing a bi-weekly local column for The Mountain Press.

Zoder maintains the award-winning blog, Homeschool Ways, where she shares her experience with homeschooling her two children.

You can connect with Adriana through her blog, www.HomeschoolWays.com, and, also, on Facebook, Twitter, Pinterest, Google+ and LinkedIn.

REVIEW REQUEST

If you enjoyed this book or you found it useful, I would be very grateful if you posted a positive review.

Please go to the book's Amazon page. There, you can write your own review and share your experience with others.

I read all reviews in order to learn from my readers.

Thank you in advance,

Adriana

Made in the USA
Middletown, DE
17 July 2016